▼As an F-117A banks left, its sleek profile is evident from the observer's angle. (Author)

This is Stealth

The F-117 and B-2 – in Color

Erik Simonsen

Greenhill Books
Presidio Press

◀ As a result of the 'Have Blue' test programme (see page 14), approval for a full-scale stealth attack aircraft was issued in November 1978, under the code-name 'Senior Trend'. Designated F-117A, the scaled-up aircraft had a wing span of 43ft 4in and a length of 65ft 11in. (Lockheed/Eric Schulzinger and Denny Lombard)

This edition of *This is Stealth: The F-117 and B-2 – in Color* first published 1992 by

Greenhill Books,
Lionel Leventhal Limited, Park House, 1 Russell Gardens, London NW11 9NN
and
Presidio Press, P.O. Box 1764, Novato, Ca. 94948, U.S.A.

British Library Cataloguing in Publication Data
Simonsen, Erik
This is Stealth: The F-117 and B-2 – in Color
I. Title
623.7
ISBN 1-85367-129-0

Library of Congress Cataloging-in-Publication Data
Simonsen, Erik.
This is Stealth: the F-117 and B-2 – in Color/by Erik Simonsen.
96p. 24cm.
ISBN 1-85367-129-0
1. F-117 (Jet fighter plane) – Pictorial works. 2. B-2 bomber – Pictorial works.
I. Title.
UG1242.F5S56 1992 92-18772
358.4'283 – dc20 CIP

► The maximum gross weight of the F-117A was now 52,500lb compared to 12,000 for the 'Have Blue' test-bed. (Author)

MANY SINCERE THANKS go out to several talented individuals and fine organizations that helped augment the author's photography within this book: outstanding photographers Tony Landis and Bill Hartenstein; fellow photographer Bernard Thouanel, from Paris; Jay Miller of Aerofax; Guy Aceto of *Air Force Magazine*; aviation expert Mike Dornheim of *Aviation Week*; the excellent photographers at Lockheed, Eric Schulzinger and Denny Lombard; Jeffrey Rhodes, public relations representative for ATF; Dave Young of Lockheed; Northrop public affairs experts C. John Amrhein, Terry Clawson and Nancy Frost; and General Electric Aircraft Engines representative Scott Vogel. Thanks go also to US Air Force public affairs officials MSgt. Bobby Shelton and Capt. Betsy Freeman. Of extreme value are the aviation illustrators who can capture that unique perspective or hypothetical aircraft that is unavailable to the camera. The talent of artist Stan Jones is evident throughout this book, and additional thanks are due to graphic illustrators Art Paredes and Chris Kato.

Erik Simonsen

Designed by DAG Publications Ltd., London.
Typset by Typesetters (Birmingham) Ltd., Warley.
Quality printing and binding by Colorcraft Limited,
6A, Victoria Centre, 15 Watson's Road, North Point, Hong Kong.

WITHOUT A DOUBT the next decade will revolutionize the aerospace industry in every aspect of technology. Low observables, materials, flight control systems, avionics, propulsion and tactics will all undergo a metamorphosis that can only be imagined at this juncture.

In the United States, several aircraft have recently emerged from the 'black world'. The USAF/Northrop B-2 Stealth Bomber is now undergoing flight tests and the USAF/Lockheed F-117A Stealth Attack Aircraft has proved its worth in Operation 'Desert Storm'. Both programmes underwent initial design and development in total secrecy, only the B-2's configuration being revealed prior to production. Stealth technology has reshaped the strike-interdiction mission – and the B-2 is a generation better than the F-117A. The cancelled US Navy A-12 Advanced Tactical Aircraft (ATA) would have represented the next generation of stealth; however, that will now be left to the new AX programme. Two superb fighters competed during the Advanced Tactical Fighter (ATF) competition, which ended on 23 April 1991. The Lockheed YF-22 was chosen to be the new USAF air superiority fighter over the Northrop YF-23. A superior blend of agility, stealth and affordability led the YF-22 into the winner's circle.

Despite the tremendous advances that have produced today's technologically superior aircraft and the proof-of-concept/trial-by-fire of several of these systems during the Gulf War, many new programmes linger amid a cloud of budgetary constraints. With the demise of the Soviet Union into the Commonwealth of Independent States (CIS), the top strategic threat to the US has changed dramatically – and current defence budgets are now reflecting that change. The F-117A will be upgraded, but there will be no re-starting of the production line. Production of the B-2 will consist of no more than 20 aircraft and the F-22 buy stands at 648. From the year 2005 to 2020 the US Navy plans to procure a total of 575 AX(N)s, the USAF following slightly later with a total of 411 land-based versions. The Multi-Role Fighter (MRF), a stealthy replacement for the venerable F-16, will begin entering the USAF inventory in 2010. Although highly capable, these programmes represent a future of fewer 'new starts' and increased 'stretch-outs' and teaming. Five teams are vying for the AX contract, the team leaders including General Dynamics, Grumman, Lockheed, McDonnell Douglas and Rockwell.

Perhaps the most striking evidence of the end of the Cold War has been realized within the US Air Force. On 1 June 1992 Strategic Air Command was deactivated and merged with Tactical Air Command into the newly formed Air Combat Command. The lessons of

'Desert Shield'/'Desert Storm' and the substantially reduced nuclear threat from Russia called for a more conventionally capable organization. This new 'lean and mean' command will make up a formidable, dual-capable strike force. Designated a 'silver bullet', the B-2 will be utilized for quick-reaction strikes and the B-1B, with an increased conventional capability, will now become the fleet workhorse. B-52Gs will remain on the inventory as conventional bombers and the B-52Hs, in the nuclear role, will carry the AGM-129A Advanced Cruise Missile (ACM). As part of this 'bomber road map', the B-1B will be armed with an array of conventional stand-off weapons. Recent 'Red Flag' exercises have shown the B-1B to be far

▼ A low sun angle enhances the faceted shape of the 'Blackjet'. The upturned empennage just aft of the platypus exhaust nozzles is visible here. (Lockheed/Eric Schulzinger and Denny Lombard)

stealthier than imagined and quite difficult to intercept. The primary stand-off weapon for the B-2 will be the Tri-Service Standoff Attack Missile (TSSAM), while the B-1B could stand off to fire the conventionally armed AGM-86C Air-Launched Cruise Missile (ALCM-C) or move in closer with additional 'smart' weapons similar to those carried by the F-117A. In other scenarios, both the B-2 and B-1B could overfly the target with gravity bombs.

Additional lessons learned during Operation 'Desert Storm' affect the reconnaissance sector. The necessary hourly tactical photo coverage and Battle Damage Assessment (BDA) was not adequate, according to field commanders. Satellites are no doubt a superb technical means for collecting data on a strategic basis; however, they obviously had problems providing data during a rapidly changing tactical scenario. For example, the surprise attack on Kuwait should not have been a surprise, while the hunt for Scud missiles, BDA and enemy troops/equipment counts (which possibly ended the war too early) all represented reconnaissance problems. Even now, during the dismantling of Iraq's offensive weapons of mass destruction, USAF U-2R/TR-1s operating on behalf of the United Nations are occasionally threatened by Iraqi SAM sites. If the recently retired SR-71 were still in service one could be assured that some, if not all, of these problems would have been greatly reduced.

Recent high-flying activities over the south-western USA and over the Pacific Ocean have offered hope that perhaps new manned and/or un-

◢ The primary mission for the F-117 (unofficially known as the 'Nighthawk' or 'Blackjet') is to enter and leave high-threat areas undetected and deliver a variety of 'smart' weapons on high-value targets. (Author)

manned reconnaissance vehicles are being flight-tested. With the premature retirement of the SR-71 and the current phasing out of the venerable RF-4, a definite need exists for a flexible recce platform for use in both the tactical and strategic theatres. Both unusual 'donuts-on-a-rope' contrail patterns and rumbling sonic booms have been noted and documented over populated areas. Project 'Aurora' has often been associated with a pulsar-engine-powered hypersonic 'wave rider' vehicle. Perhaps, with such tests flights shifting to daylight hours and new construction facilities being reported at Beale AFB, California, a 'loosening up' of the programme may be imminent. Receiving less attention is the probable testing of a stealthy tactical reconnaissance aircraft (TR-3), capable of operating autonomously yet also in close co-ordination with the F-117A, F-15E, B-1B and B-2 as they launch their stand-off 'smart' weapons or depart from the target area. A TR-3 type aircraft would also be utilized for immediate post-strike analysis.

If eventually revealed, these programmes will confirm that American industrial ingenuity and that spark of innovation are still alive. And, more importantly, we can learn from our lessons and move swiftly in the right direction. Stealth technology is here to stay: it now represents 13 per cent of the Pentagon's budget. Stealth equates to survivability: in air-to-air combat, a stealthy aircraft gets the first look, the

▶ Drag rudders on the B-2's trailing outer wings can be activated symmetrically or asymmetrically, for speed and yaw control respectively. (Bill Hartenstein/ Author)

first shot and the first kill. In the air-to-ground mode a stealthy aircraft is a stable launch platform with no need for jinking manoeuvres, allowing higher attack altitudes for increased accuracy – and a stealthy aircraft can destroy vital air defences, thus enabling non-stealthy aircraft to be more effective in their subsequent attack.

Tracking the exotic aircraft of today from behind a camera is an inspiring experience. It is an exciting period to capture on film. In every aspect, the progress of the aviation and aerospace industries during the past 20 years has been spectacular. Whether a commercial airplane or a supersonic fighter, the subject's inherent beauty is

there to capture. Photography is quite unique in one respect: once an image is frozen in time and the photographer has created a powerful shape splashed in colour, the creative process need not be finished. The photographer can re-examine the negative or slide, shift the mood with modified colour, change the background and/or foreground or ex- pose additional images within the frame in a continuum of creativity. Within this book we peer through the camera lens and 'render on canvas' the power and grace of today's aircraft – and then, with the same medium, visu- alize what might lie ahead in the fascinating yet aesthetic world of aero- space.

◀ The evolving sophistication of stealth aircraft owes its origins to the Lockheed A-12/SR-71 Blackbird family of 'first generation' operational stealth aircraft. (Author)

▼ During November 1975, under the code-name 'Have Blue', the XST project was initiated. Lockheed and Northrop each produced full-scale RCS models. Although the competition was close, Lockheed prevailed and went on to produce two flying test-beds. Lockheed's 'Have Blue', shown here, had a wing span of 22ft and a length of 38ft and weighed 12,000lb. (Lockheed)

C78-1005-16

HAVE BLUE GENERAL ARRANGEMENT

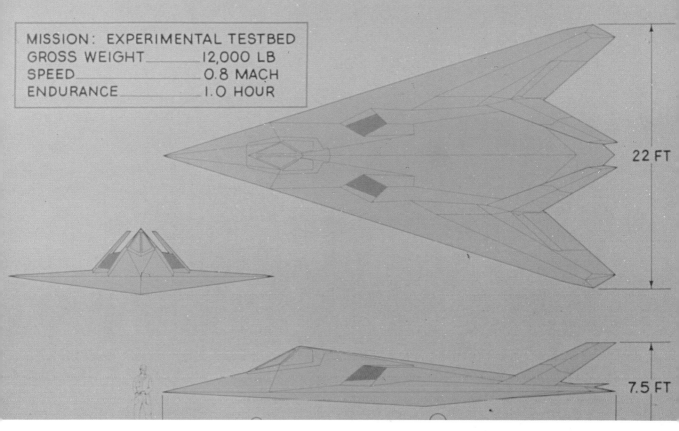

MISSION: EXPERIMENTAL TESTBED
GROSS WEIGHT_____12,000 LB
SPEED_____0.8 MACH
ENDURANCE_____1.0 HOUR

22 FT

7.5 FT

▲ The Lockheed 'Have Blue' prototype featured inwardly canted vertical fins and was used to establish an RCS baseline against ground-based and airborne radar threats. (Lockheed)

▶ In this recently released illustration, Northrop's XST design features a faceted fuselage with a single intake above and just aft of the cockpit. The actual full-scale RCS model, however, had vertical fins that were slightly canted inward. (Northrop)

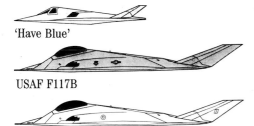

'Have Blue'

USAF F117B

RAF F-117C

◀ In 1979 a full-scale wooden mockup was constructed at Lockheed's Skunk Works before the full-scale development (FSD) vehicles went into production. (Lockheed)

◀▼After shipment from Lockheed's Burbank, California, facility via a C-5, an FSD vehicle is reassembled by Lockheed technicians at the secret Groom Lake test area. (Lockheed)

▲ To test the radar cross section (RCS) of the F-117's faceted design, Lockheed used pole models at its New Mexico site beginning in 1978 and continued at Antelope Valley, California, radar range after 1988. (Lockheed)

▼ Behind camouflaged netting, Lockheed technicians prepare an FSD aircraft for flight testing. Note engine exhaust area panels removed. (Lockheed)

◀ An excellent view of the first flight test aircraft (No. 780) over the Groom Lake test range. The five FSD aircraft were designated Scorpion 1 through Scorpion 5 and the number 1 aircraft was the only F-117 to be painted both in a desert camouflage and in a flat grey. Later, the TAC commander ordered that all aircraft be painted black. (USAF)

▲ Scorpion 5 (No. 784) conducts a weapons separation test with a GBU-27 over the Groom Lake range. Note the orange camera pods under the left wing to record bomb release. (USAF)

▼ A special cockpit ladder was developed to protect the aircraft's sensitive skin and leading edge. (Author)

F-117 attack aircraft

◀ The F-117's twin weapons bays can each carry a single 2,000lb air-to-ground weapon internally. (Tony Landis)

▼ 'Have Blue' had a leading-edge wing sweep of 72.5°, which reduced performance; full-scale development (FSD) F-117As had a wing sweep that was reduced to 67.5°, which resulted in a better all-round performance and a slower landing speed. (Author)

▶ Unlike the prototype's, the F-117's vertical stabilizers are canted outward with a height of 12ft 5in. (Author)

▼ YF-117A full-scale development (FSD) aircraft No. 783 taxis at Edwards Air Force Base, California. Most FSD aircraft were not equipped with a fully activated weapons delivery system. The remaining FSD aircraft are currently used for training. (Author)

F-117 attack aircraft

◄ Another view of FSD air vehicle No. 783 indicates that it has probably been updated with the new graphite/thermoplastic vertical fins. (Author)

► The F-117's visual profile changes dramatically with the viewing angle. (Author)

▼ FSD aircraft are used to test and integrate new avionics and instrumentation upgrades into the production aircraft. (Author)

◀ Ninety per cent of the F-117's low observability is attributable to its faceted shape; the remaining 10 per cent is provided by RAM applied selectively, IR shielding and special paint coatings. (Author)

◀▼The FLIR (forward looking infra-red) sensor unit is located just below the cockpit windscreen. Faceted shaping of the nose is designed to reflect away or disperse incoming radar waves. (Author)

▼ The single-seat cockpit is generally considered roomy and provides 5in of side-to-side head movement for the pilot. (Author)

▲In addition to having a faceted design, the cockpit's glass panels are coated with gold film laminate RAM. (Author)

▼A good low-angle view of aircraft No. 842, showing the four specially developed, faceted-shaped, electrically conductive plastic pitot tubes. A 'voting system' ensures that the correct data are fed into the quadruple-redundant fly-by-wire flight control system. (Author)

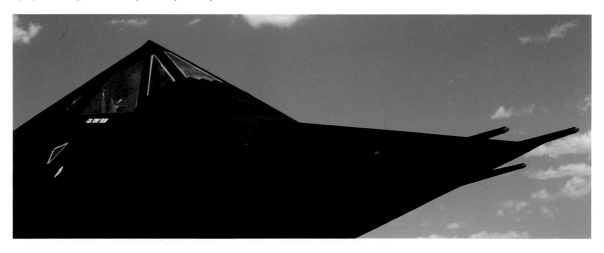

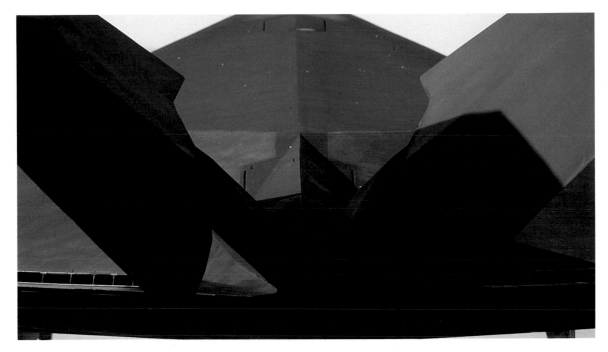

▲ A slightly elevated view from the rear reveals the exhaust nozzles. Also visible here are the all-moving breakpoints for the vertical fins and the drag 'chute doors. (Author)

▼ The flattened exhaust nozzles are divided into twelve sections for each engine. Cool ambient air is mixed into the exhaust gases to reduce the infra-red signature. In addition, the exhaust passes over heat-absorbing tiles similar to those developed for the Space Shuttle. (Tony Landis)

 A side view of the F-117A reveals the saw-tooth effect around the cockpit windscreen and the intake RAM screen. (Author)

◀ The public takes a look at the mystery 'Blackjet' at Andrews AFB, Maryland. (Author)

CAPT DAVE FRANCIS

▶ With a waning moon above an F-117A taxis under cover of darkness. (Author)

▼ Because of the F-117A's relatively high landing speed, the drag 'chute is used on every landing, thus saving wear and tear on the carbon-fibre brakes. (Author)

F-117 attack aircraft

◀ A telephoto-enhanced image of the sun illuminates the 'Nighthawk's' unique profile. (Author)

▲ Under a setting desert sun, FSD air vehicle No. 783 (officially designated YF-117A) moves toward the Edwards AFB hangar area. (Author)

▼ The twin vertical stabilizers are canted outwards approximately 30° from the vertical. (Lockheed/Eric Schulzinger)

◀ The hyraulically steerable nose gear retracts forwards. Note the landing light. (Author)

▶ This photograph provides a good view of the F-117A's cockpit. The HUD (with helmet) and ACES II ejection seat are clearly visible. (Bernard Thouanel)

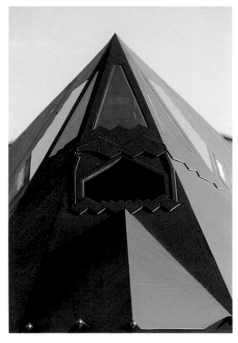

◀◀ Side-view detail of the main landing gear. Part of the upgrades destined for the F-117 will include improved brakes. (Author)

◀ A head-on view of the second production aircraft, No. 786, during a visit to Davis-Monthan AFB, Arizona. (Author)

▶ The Nighthawks of Desert Storm. During the early-morning hours of 17 January 1991, an F-117A releases a 2,000lb laser-guided bomb near Baghdad. (Stan Jones)

▼ A 'Blackjet' pilot goes through pre-flight checks at a Saudi Arabian desert base during Operation 'Desert Storm'. (USAF)

35

▼ A small visual profile is evident as an F-117A takes off from a secret Saudi operating base during 'Desert Storm'. It is believed that 44 F-117s and 60 pilots flew 1,271 combat missions from Saudi bases during the Gulf War. (USAF)

◀ From inside a stone-lined revetment at an undisclosed Saudi base, an F-117A prepares to taxi. (USAF)

▶ An F-117A approaches a tanker during a 'Desert Storm' ferry flight. The two operational squadrons and the training unit based at the Tonopah Test Range Airfield in Nevada were deployed to Saudi Arabia. (Mike Dornheim)

▶▼ The refuelling receptacle on the F-117A is located aft of the cockpit. A small light on top on the canopy faces rearwards to illuminate the receptacle during night operations. (Mike Dornheim)

◀ 'Nighthawk' No. 790, silhouetted against darkening skies. (Author)

▼ An F-117A taxis out of its Saudi air base revetment. (USAF)

◤ As the sun sets, the F-117's day is just beginning. The F-117A production run consisted of 59 production aircraft and five FSD or YF-117As, for a total of 64. (Author)

◤ The F-117's crosshairs have been slewed on to the Iraqi Air Force's Central Command HQ, which now becomes the DMPI, or 'designated mean point of impact'. Moments later a 2,000lb GBU-27 precision-guided munition went through the roof ventilation shaft. (DoD)

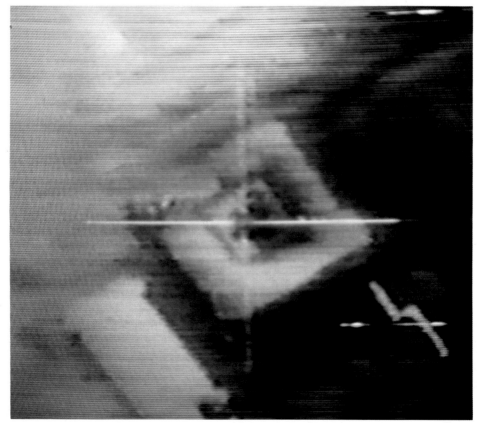

▶ A KC-135Q and an F-117A hook up for routine twilight air-to-air refuelling. (Lockheed/Eric Schulzinger and Denny Lombard)

▶ The F-117A is described by pilots as 'smoother than the F-15 in handling qualities'. Although not designed as a high-performance air-to-air fighter, the F-117 has roll rate of 180° per second and can pull 6g manoeuvres. (Author)

F-117 attack aircraft

▲ During Operation 'Desert Storm', a typical mission included planning (3–4 hours), sortie to target and return (average 5.5 hours), time in enemy air space (30–45 minutes) and debriefing (2 hours). (Author)

▶ In the wake of the Gulf War, the F-117A was a huge attraction at the 1991 Paris Air Show. A GBU-10 Paveway II is seen on display with the aircraft. (Bernard Thouanel)

▼ Aircraft No. 830 prepares to shut down engines and systems upon arrival at Le Bourget for the 1991 Paris Air Show. (Benard Thouanel)

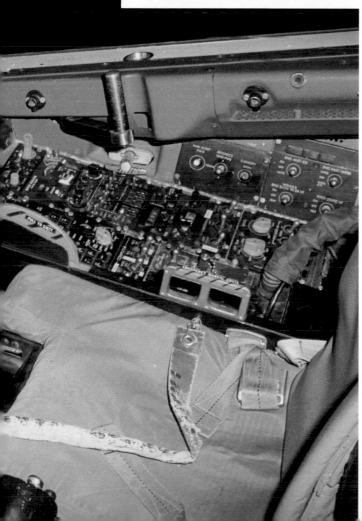

◀ The instrument panel of the F-117 as it matured was a combination of old and new. Some off-the-shelf items were utilized, such as the multifunctional display indicators (MDIs), HUD, engine read-outs, fuel gauges, control stick and throttles from the F/A-18. (Hugh Morgan)

▲ During mid-1991 the second YF-117A (FSD No. 781) was retired and flown to the US Air Force Museum at Dayton, Ohio. This is a view of the main instrument panel. More recently updated instruments have been removed for security reasons. (Hugh Morgan)

▶ A long-awaited close look at the current F-117A cockpit. **See also overleaf.** Of particular interest are the large MFDs (Multi-Function Displays) for the FLIR (forward-looking infra-red) and DLIR (downward-looking infra-red) that are essential to the aircraft's night-attack mission. Located just below the HUD is the key pad for entering and calling up HUD in-flight data. Note the folding glare shields. (Lockheed)

◀ As of mid-1992, 20 aircraft in the fleet of 56 have received a number of cockpit improvements. Under the Offensive Capability Improvement Program (OCIP), F-117 pilots now have a Digital Tactical Display (DTD), automatic throttles for mission cruise control and an upgraded mission computer. (Lockheed/Eric Schulzinger and Denny Lombard)

▶ A close view of a returning 'Desert Storm' veteran reveals the FLIR sensor and mission markings. (Tony Landis)

◀ An F-117A returning from the Gulf War touches down at Nellis AFB, Nevada. Note the GBU 27 bomb mission symbols just below the cockpit. (Tony Landis)

▶ As a 'Blackjet' taxis out to the Nellis runway, a Royal Norwegian Air Force F-16A 'Red Flag' participant passes overhead. (Tony Landis)

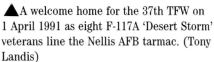▲A welcome home for the 37th TFW on
1 April 1991 as eight F-117A 'Desert Storm'
veterans line the Nellis AFB tarmac. (Tony
Landis)

◀In an age of low observables and low-
profile markings, nose art has now changed
to weapons bay door art. Here artwork
entitled 'Final Verdict' is visible on aircraft
No. 814. (Tony Landis)

▶ Col. Al Whitley, Commander of the 37th
TFW, flew the 'Toxic Avenger', which was
aircraft No. 813. The weapons bay doors are
hinged along the aircraft centreline – and,
once these are opened, the bomb mount
lowers the weapon into the airstream.
Spoilers activated in front of the bay assure
a clean release. (Tony Landis)

▶ F-117A No. 825, 'Mad–Max'. (Tony
Landis)

▶ F-117A No. 808, 'Thor'. (Tony Landis)

▶ This cutaway of the F-117A shows the location of the cockpit avionics, fuel cells, F404-GE-F1D2 engines and weapons bays. Lightweight composites account for only 5 per cent of aircraft weight, with aluminium comprising the majority of the material. This ratio is currently shifting, however, with the introduction of composites in the airframe improvement programme. (Art Paredes)

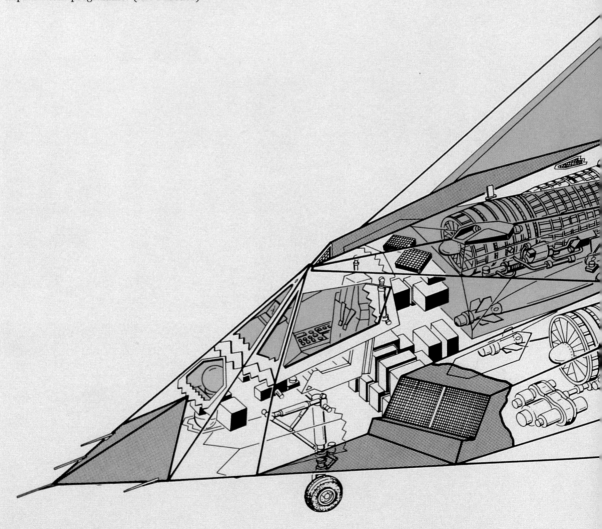

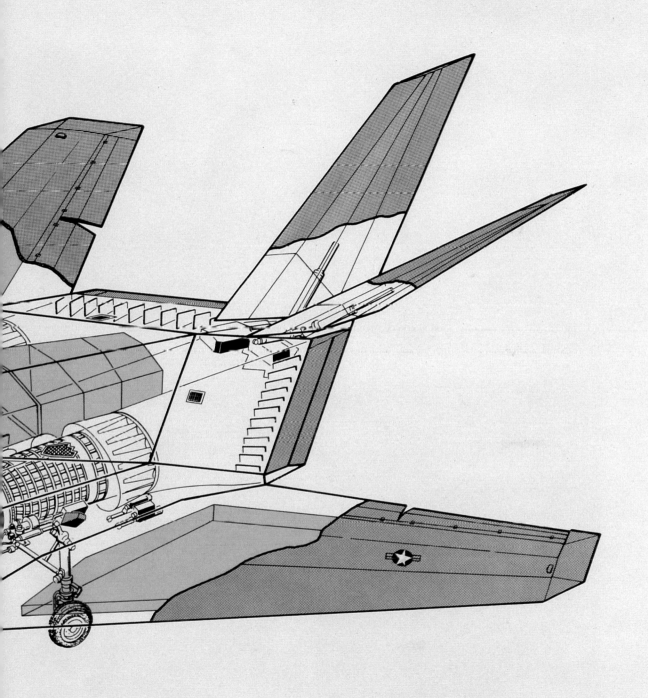

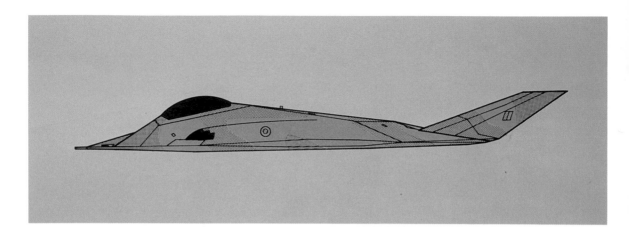

▲Royal Air Force pilots have been flying the F-117 for several years, and there have been rumours of RAF procurement of the aircraft. With no impending restart of the line for the USAF, however, it is unlikely that such will occur. In addition to the internal improvements, an F-117B version could possibly sport a bubble canopy (based on F-22 ATF technology) and, with a redesigned intake, allow the removal of the RAM screen. (Art Paredes)

▲ 415th Tactical Fighter Squadron ('Night Stalkers') patch.

▶▲ 417th Tactical Fighter Training Squadron ('Bandits') patch.

▶ 37th Tactical Fighter Wing patch.

◀◀ 'Ghost Riders' squadron marking on F-117A No. 814. (John Dzurica)

◀ 416th Tactical Fighter Squadron ('Ghost Riders') patch.

▲ We must assume that, within the CIS (Commonwealth of Independent States), formerly the Soviet Union, 'black' aircraft programmes are continuing. This is a 'first generation' faceted-design stealth aircraft postulated by the Testors Corporation. (Author)

▶▲ A model concept depicting the USAF/Northrop B-2 at altitude shortly before photographs of the actual B-2 were made available. (Author)

▶ A bird's-eye view of the 22 November 1988 roll-out of the B-2 at Northrop's Palmdale Facility. (Bill Hartenstein)

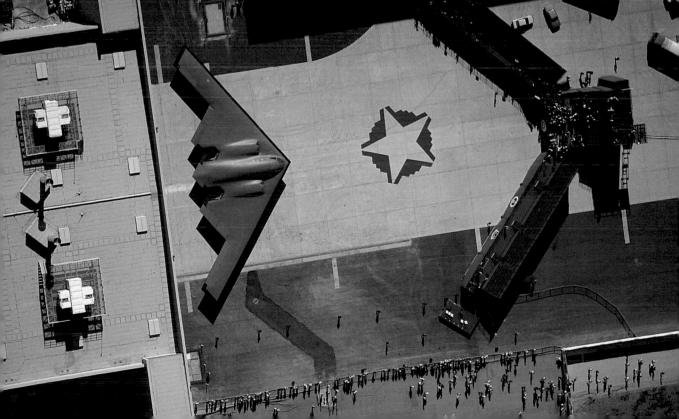

▲ On 17 July 1989, at 6.37 a.m. PDT, the No. 1 B-2 Advanced Technology Bomber lifted off from the Palmdale, California, runway for the first time. (Northrop)

▲▶ The B-2 production line at Northrop's Palmdale Site 4 final assembly facility. The plastic and special padding are for security and for the protection of sensitive materials. (Northrop)

▶ B-2 No. 1 (left) and No. 2 (right), parked outside Northrop's specially constructed Edwards AFB flight test facility. (Northrop)

▲ The B-2 utilizes virtually every stealth technique within its design and operation. Stealthiness is achieved through shape, materials/RAM, the absence of a vertical tail, embedded engines, an internal weapons bay, IR shielding, ECM, inlet positioning/RAM, low reflective/low contrast paints, mission tactics and night flying. (Author)

◄ Advances in technology have allowed Northrop's design team to shift away from a faceted design (as in the F-117A) and towards a curvilinear shape. (Northrop)

▼ A trailing static cone is housed in a temporary support structure near the centre tail section of the B-2. Trailing behind a test aircraft, the cone provides a neutral source of static air pressure. On a normal airframe such devices usually emanate from the tip of the vertical stabilizer. (Northrop)

With a limited number of B-2s (15–20) on the inventory, the 97 Rockwell B-1Bs currently in service will take on a more prominent conventional role in Air Combat Command. (Author)

In addition to various low observable techniques, the B-1B effectively uses terrain-masking to avoid detection. The B-1B has been optimized for high subsonic penetration at very low altitudes. (Author)

▲ The handling qualities of the B-2 were reported to be very stable behind the KC-10. Note the upper surface detail, including the inlet's saw-tooth edge and lower lip that prevents tubulent air from entering. (Northrop)

B-2 bomber aircraft

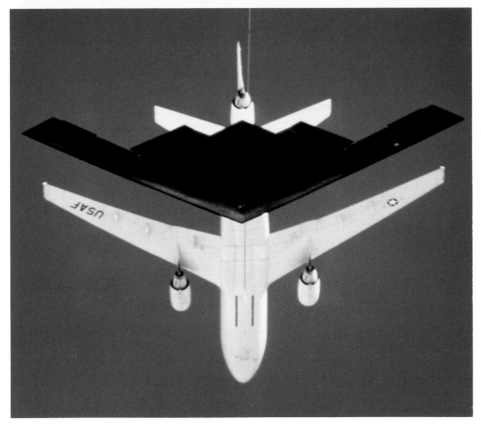

▲ A remarkably different aspect of the B-2 is apparent from head-on: minimal frontal area is presented to the observer compared to the planform view. Note the 'day-glo' orange sections that are temporarily affixed to the leading and trailing edges of the aircraft. (Bill Hartenstein)

◀ The conventional and unconventional: the KC-10 and B-2 as viewed from an F-16B chase aircraft. (USAF)

▲ A rear three-quarter view of the B-2 emphasizes the very low visual profile of the aircraft. (USAF)

▶ The planform of the B-2 reveals its curvilinear shape as well as its saw-tooth trailing edge. Noteworthy also is the design configuration to shield the engine exhaust. (USAF)

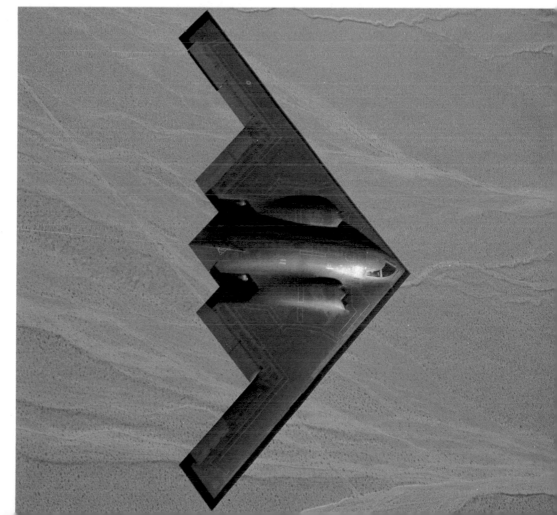

▲ The wing span of the B-2 is 172ft and the length 69ft. Unrefuelled range is approximately 6,500 miles; one in-flight refuelling can extend that to 10,000 miles. (USAF)

▶ A view from behind the seats of the No. 1 B-2 reveals a 'glass' cockpit and fighter-like control sticks. Although the aircraft is currently flying with a crew of two, facilities for a third crew member are available should future missions require one. (Northrop)

B-2 bomber aircraft

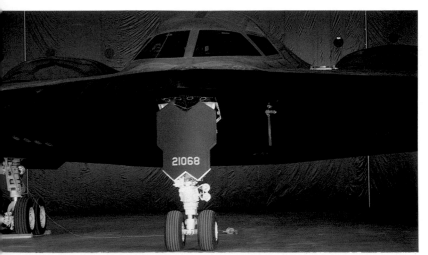

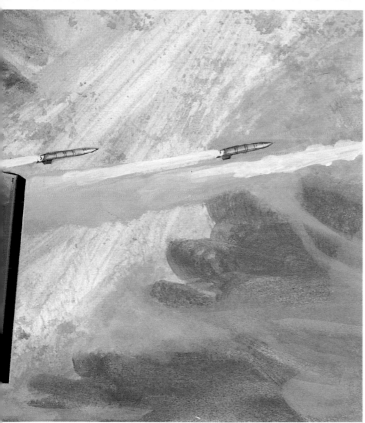

◀▲ A good, detailed look at B-2 AV-3 in an Edwards AFB hangar, October 1991. (Author)

◀ This artist's rendering depicts what the B-2 might have looked like on a future mission launching the SRAM (Short Range Attack Missile) II. The SRAM II was cancelled in 1991, however. (Stan Jones)

▲ Things that go bump in the night! Under the cloak of darkness, a B-2 moves out of the paint hangar at Northrop's Site 4 Palmdale Facility. Payload can consist of up to 50,000lb of conventional or nuclear weapons, which would include precision-guided stand-off missiles, 'smart' bombs, gravity bombs and the ACM (Advanced Cruise Missile). (Northrop)

◀▲ The B-2's main landing gear was extensively tested at Boeing's Seattle facility. The main wheel wells are each covered by a single large door. (Author)

▲ 'No. 21068' affixed to the nose gear door indicates that this is B-2 Air Vehicle No. 3 (AV-3). (Author)

◀ The cockpit windscreen gives the crew over 200° of panoramic visibility. (Author)

▲ The automatic blow-in doors on top of each engine inlet allow additional air to be fed to the engines during taxiing and take-off. (General Electric)

▼ B-2 AV-1 on static display during 'Stealth Week' at Andrews AFB, Maryland. The aircraft's autumn 1991 public début followed the B-2's first cross-country flight. (Jay Miller/Author)

▶ Activated drag rudders are visible as the B-2 comes in for a landing at Edwards AFB, California. (Bill Hartenstein/Author)

▼ A KC-10A and a B-2 engage in refuelling tests over the Mojave Desert. (USAF)

◀ Radar-reflective
orange markings
temporarily affixed
to the B-2 enable
ground tracking
stations to monitor
the aircraft more
easily. (Bill
Hartenstein)

▲ From a satellite's point of view: tracking the B-2 on the Palmdale taxi strip. (Bill Hartenstein)

▶ As of 20 April 1992 the three B-2 test aircraft at Edwards AFB had accumulated 475.5 hours in 110 test-flights. Here we have a rare detailed view of the B-2's underside. (Northrop)

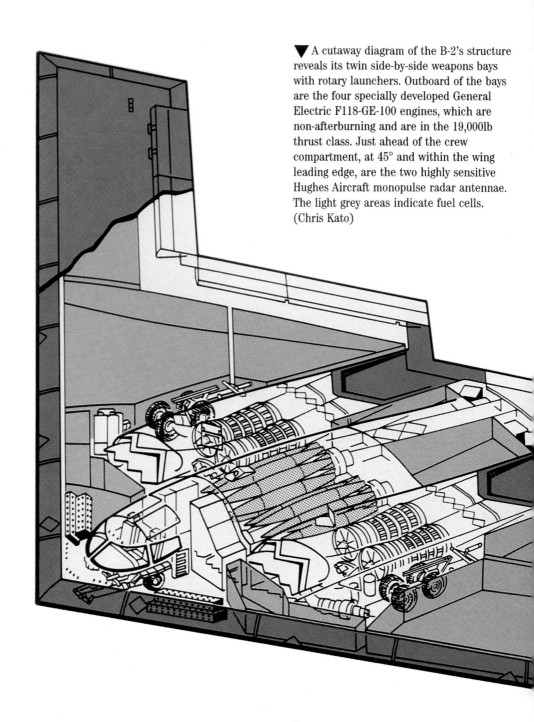

▼ A cutaway diagram of the B-2's structure reveals its twin side-by-side weapons bays with rotary launchers. Outboard of the bays are the four specially developed General Electric F118-GE-100 engines, which are non-afterburning and are in the 19,000lb thrust class. Just ahead of the crew compartment, at 45° and within the wing leading edge, are the two highly sensitive Hughes Aircraft monopulse radar antennae. The light grey areas indicate fuel cells. (Chris Kato)

▲ Into the heat of the night: a B-2 take-off at Palmdale. (Bill Hartenstein/Author)

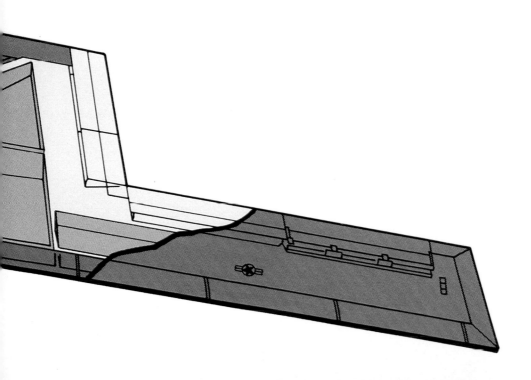

◀ On 9 August 1991 the Pentagon moved the F-22 programme into full-scale development. The total combined value of the F-22 to prime contractor (Lockheed) and engine contractor (Pratt & Whitney) is estimated at $12 billion, for 648 aircraft. (YF-22 Photographic Team)

▲ The first F-22 is scheduled to enter service in the year 2002 and will gradually supersede the F-15 Eagle as the primary USAF air superiority fighter. (YF-22 Photographic Team)

▼ Of primary importance was the incorporation of agility, power, close-in/stand-off air combat capability and stealthiness into the ATF design. The Lockheed/Boeing/General Dynamics team met or exceeded these requirements with the YF-22. (Author)

This is Stealth

Although the Northrop/McDonnell Douglas YF-23 lost in its bid for the ATF contract, the design was considered to be an excellent blend of agility and the latest in stealth technology. (Northrop)

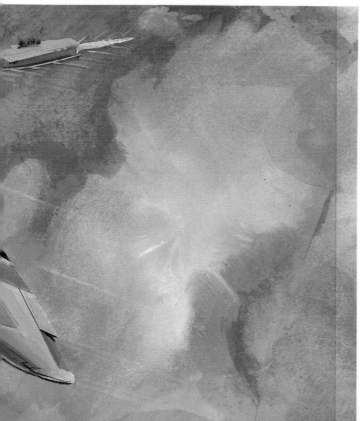

◀ This AX artist's concept features a delta planform and, unlike the A-12, twin vertical fins. These will sacrifice some low observability, although substantial savings will be achieved with a less sophisticated flight control system. Such a strategy concurs with the Navy's balanced design approach with regard to speed, range, agility and survivability. (Stan Jones)

▲ The cancelled two-seat General Dynamics/McDonnell Douglas A-12 Avenger was being developed to replace the ageing US Navy/ Grumman A-6 Intruder. Its triangular planform, featuring recessed inlets on the lower wing leading edge and IR-shielded 'louvred' exhaust nozzles, was to have been very stealthy. (Author)

◀ According to the Navy, the AX will be a high-subsonic or faster attack aircraft with a combat radius of approximately 700 nautical miles. Payload specifications call for about 4,500–8,000lb of ordnance, with provision for at least two air-to-air missiles. (Stan Jones)

▲ A team headed by Lockheed and including General Dynamics and Boeing is offering a derivative of the USAF F-22 ATF as an AX candidate. (Stan Jones)

◀ A major design change in the Lockheed Naval derivative of the F-22 ATF is the inclusion of variable-sweep wings for carrier landing suitability; the supersonic dash capability is retained. (Lockheed)

▲ The stealthy unmanned Lockheed D-21 reconnaissance drones usually operated at an altitude of about 85,000ft, at approximately Mach 3.2 to 3.4. Its unusual shape evident, this GTD-21B is among 22 drones in retirement at Davis-Monthan AFB, Arizona. (Author)

▼ A rearward-facing camera mounted on the M-12 records a D-21 launch/separation.

A recently released photograph showing a Lockheed D-21 atop its M-12 mother ship at a 'remote' Lockheed facility. This mid-1960s vintage photo depicts the early 'piggy-back' launch configuration from a modified SR-71. Later in the D-21 reconnaissance programme the drones were pylon-launched from a B-52 and brought up to engine ignition speed by means of a ventral booster. (Lockheed)

▼ Early in the programme, the D-21 RPV (remotely piloted vehicle) was launched from a modified SR-71, designated M-12. (Lockheed)

▲ Designed as a follow-on to the Boeing AGM-86B ALCM, the AGM-129A ACM (Advanced Cruise Missile) enhances the survivability of both the launch aircraft and missile with increased range and stealthiness. (Author)

▶ A stealthy tactical reconnaissance/BDA (Battle Damage Assessment) aircraft could appear in the form of this concept, sometimes referred to as the TR-3 or U-3A (the designation TR may be dropped by Air Combat Command). Note the B-2 type inlets and drag rudders. (Stan Jones)

▶ This unmanned 'Aurora' concept is contour-optimized to land and take off in an inverted mode (note inverted national insignia). At a predetermined point after take-off, a roll manoeuvre is initiated before the aircraft goes hypersonic. (Stan Jones)

▼ The General Dynamics ACM has forward-swept wings for cruise efficiency and an off-centre ventral fin (IR shield), and features the extensive use of RAM. (Author)

▲A larger hypersonic manned 'Aurora' could perform strategic reconnaissance missions at altitudes of 100,000–120,000ft. (Stan Jones)

▶Entering the USAF inventory around 2010, the stealthy MRF (Multi-Role Fighter) would gradually replace the F-16. The mission-adaptive canards assist in supersonic cruise and increase agility during close in air-to-air combat. (Stan Jones)

▼According to Northrop's Chief B-2 Test Pilot Bruce Hinds, in the event of a multiple failure in both engines one and two (left nacelle) or in both three and four (right nacelle), the computerized flight control system will automatically activate the drag rudders to compensate for asymmetric thrust. This action is initiated and completed before a human could begin to react. (Northrop)